Boxing's Ten Commandments

1
Fight from the boxer's stance with rhythm

2
Learn to move skillfully in all directions

3
Know and master your range

4
Obey the laws of punching and punch power

5
Make the jab your best punch

6
Master the mechanics of the major punches

7
Master the defenses against each punch
and know how to counter every attack

8
Angle in and out on different lines

9
Blend and master offensive and defensive skills
through focused sparring drills

10
Follow a plan every round —
be it workout, sparring or competition

Boxing's Ten Commandments
Essential Training for the Sweet Science

Alan Lachica
with Doug Werner

Photography by Doug Werner

Tracks Publishing
San Diego, California

Boxing's Ten Commandments
Alan Lachica with Doug Werner

Tracks Publishing
140 Brightwood Avenue
Chula Vista, CA 91910
619-476-7125
tracks@cox.net
www.startupsports.com

Copyright © 2007 by Doug Werner
10 9 8 7 6 5 4

Publisher's Cataloging-in-Publication

    Lachica, Alan.
       Boxing's ten commandments : essential training for
    the sweet science / Alan Lachica with Doug Werner ;
    photography by Doug Werner.
       p. cm.
    Includes index.
    LCCN 2007924994
    ISBN-13: 978-1-884654-28-2
    ISBN-10: 1-884654-28-2

    1. Boxing–Training.   I. Werner, Doug, 1950-
II. Title.

GV1137.6.L33 2007   796.83
                         QBI07-600100

Dedicated
to
Tony Lachica
and the guys of Bulldog Boxing Gym

Special thanks
to
Tony Lachica
Steve Smith
Josh Hanson
Ben Holder
Neil Mitchell
Debbie Brock
Alex Brock
Lynne Lachica
Phyllis Carter

Special mention
to
Savanna Lachica
Camryn Lachica

Contents

Introduction

This boxing guide sorts and explains essential technique and knowledge that every boxer should know. This information is distilled into ten major points or commandments. Vital points are illustrated with hundreds of sequential images. Furthermore, fundamental skills are woven into a progression of drills that hone

 technique in increasingly complex, demanding and realistic fighting situations. A major goal of this book is to help readers grow from a process and react mentality to seeing and reacting — developing the reflexes of a complete boxer.

Why the book is different

This is a serious boxer's guide. Not to be confused with boxing for fitness or boxing for fans. *Boxing's Ten Commandments* lays out and knits together major areas of boxing training that are either briefly noted, poorly explained or overlooked in other guides. The reader will find up to date information regarding boxing essentials such as stance, footwork and punching. Knowledge about counterpunching and creating angles may be old hat to insiders at the gym, but has never been documented page by page like this.

It is assumed that readers are familiar with basic boxing technique and training. Our first two boxing books, *Boxer's Start-Up* and *Fighting Fit*, cover beginning and intermediate boxing and we recommend that those new to the game start there.

Special note
This guide is about boxing related workout plans. Weight training, stretching, running and nutrition — all vital to success — are not mentioned. This book deals exclusively with the Sweet Science.

Stance and rhythm

**First Commandment:
Fight from the boxer's stance with rhythm**

A classic on guard stance is the foundation upon which everything is built.

Even the great Roy Jones Jr. learned how to keep his hands up and elbows in before gravitating to his famous left arm down style. A classic on guard stance gives you the ability to punch and defend at the same time. And in a nutshell, that's boxing! — being able to throw and defend simultaneously.

Your stance should allow for a sideways facing upper body (shows less target with more rotational power) and a slightly open lower body with your front toes in line with your back heel. This allows for a quicker and longer right hand and better balance.

Stance and rhythm

Building a stance

The spine should be angled a little forward. This activates the core muscles of your trunk. This is the ideal ready and athletic stance to be in. Look at top tennis, football and baseball players at the moment before they react. You will see that they assume this posture. Boxers should do the same!

It goes like this:

Align the toe of your lead foot with the heel of your back foot. Angle your spine slightly forward. Position your head behind your lead foot. Bring your hands up with the lead hand a bit in front of your lead shoulder. The back hand should be slightly in front of, or next to, the chin. Place your elbows in front of your body pointing down with forearms parallel. Your chin is down as if you're holding a tennis ball between it and your chest.

Good and bad — An upright stance with a narrow base (right) is unstable.

A good way to build your stance is in front of a mirror. Begin with your feet together, then step with your lead foot slightly more than a regular step toward the mirror. This should pull your back heel off the ground. Next, turn your shoulders so that they're square to the side wall. Turn your head so that you're looking at the mirror. Bring your arms around until they rest in front of you. Note that your shoulders remain turned. Slightly tilt your spine toward the mirror. Keep your head behind your front foot. Your weight should be equally distributed over each foot.

There's some disagreement regarding fist clinching. Some coaches say a hand should be loose and made into a fist only before impact. Others say hands should stay fisted from bell to bell. I believe they should be free. I liken it to a cat ready to pounce. Its joints are free but muscles are ready to explode.

There's also some debate on where to stare. I like looking at the upper chest area. This allows you to look at your opponent from head to feet.

Long and short rhythm

Rhythm should be addressed along with stance. Physics 101 states that a body in motion tends to stay in motion and a body at rest tends to stay at rest. That's why a shortstop in baseball moves his feet before the batter starts his swing. He's ready and doesn't have to create start-up strength. Rhythm makes it much easier to react offensively or defensively. You give your opponent a moving target difficult to hit. He has to time you and get in your rhythm. In other words, he has to think about hitting you.

Although there are several types, long and short rhythm are the most popular. Most people think of Mohammed Ali when talking about long rhythm. Short rhythm is associated with Joe Frazier. Basically a long rhythm is moving in, out and side to side with total body movement. Short rhythm is more side to side (to avoid straight punches) with a little in and out and a lot of head movement. Short rhythm is brisker than long rhythm. That's because you're usually moving forward, spending more time in the boxing zone where you can get hit.

Long rhythm — Back and forth total body movement.

Short rhythm — Side to side with head movement.

2

Second Commandment:
Learn to move skillfully in all directions

A boxer must learn to move forward, back, left and right effortlessly.

A boxer's most overlooked asset is his feet. They can keep you out of a bad situation. They keep you balanced and ready to react offensively or defensively. Good footwork is essential in ring generalship. Learning how to fight moving in all four directions gives you tremendous advantage over an opponent who cannot.

Footwork should be one of the first elements in your workout. It's fundamental to all your offensive and defense maneuvers. Simply put, the foot closest to the direction you are going moves first. Stay in your stance while moving to maintain balance and to stay protected. Keep your feet close to the ground. Small steps are usually sufficient. Always push off and slide the second foot. This keeps you from over-stepping. Overstepping will throw you off balance and slows reaction time. If you take big steps and your opponent does something unexpected, you have to get that foot down before you can react. By sliding the second foot, you can react offensively or defensively instantly.

Keeping your movement efficient keeps you moving quickly and powerfully. Remember, maintaining a slightly wider than shoulder-width stance promotes smaller steps. Smaller steps promote quicker reactions.

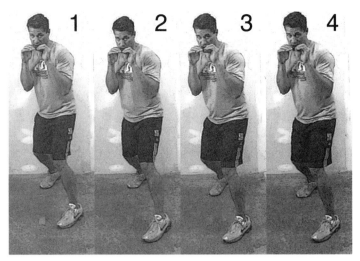

Stepping and dragging forward.

Stepping and dragging backward.

Stepping and dragging to his right.

Stepping and dragging to his left.

Footwork

Box drill — Stepping and dragging forward, to his left, back and to his right.

Circle drill — Small inside steps and larger outside steps around a set point, bag or opponent. Pivots around a stationary lead foot are utilized to help complete the circular path (see 9 and 10 above and pages 24 and 25).

Pivoting — Sweeping around a stationary lead foot.

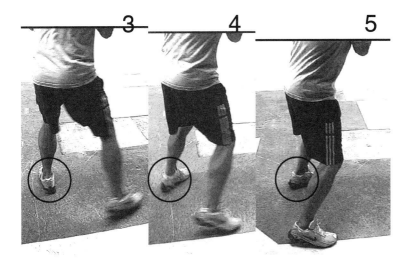

3 Range

Third Commandment:
Know and master your range

A boxer's range should be 2-4 inches outside his opponent's reach.

The better you become at relaxing, the closer you should be — but still just out of his reach. This helps in several ways. Your opponent must step to hit you. This gives you an extra fraction of a second to react either offensively or defensively. And you will not "freak out" every time your opponent punches at you because you know his punch will fall short. Lastly, it keeps the pressure on him.

After all, it's the perception of being hit that tires most boxers. Every now and then slip a punch. This closes the distance and gives you a good chance at countering him with a surprise attack. Remember, if he's out of range to hit you, chances are you're out of range to hit him.

It's common for novice boxers to stand either too far from or too close to their opponent. Standing too far away allows your opponent to rest and limits what you can do offensively. Standing too close doesn't give you enough time to react and plan an intelligent offensive attack. It's more of the rock 'em sock 'em, robot approach.

Finding his range —
Taking a half step back
from the end of his
opponent's reach.

Even if you're giving up reach in order to infight, standing at the end of your opponent's punch (impact position) isn't the way to do it. Taking two to give one isn't a fair trade unless you're a tremendous power puncher and your opponent is not.

Mike Tyson won most of his fights because of his opponents' perception of getting hit. He didn't go out there and throw 100 punches a round. It was that constant pressure just outside his opponents' reach that broke them down. Every now and then, he would make them miss by slipping and making them pay. He mastered range! It may have seemed like he was always in range to be hit, but he wasn't. Instead he was at his range, ready to pounce when the moment was right!

Mastering range enables you to know when to engage and when not to. This is a very big part of ring generalship. Staying just outside an opponent's range usually causes him to pursue you. This is important because no matter what style you use, it's easier to hit somebody if you know where he's going to be.

You can set traps by engaging your opponent when he's not ready. You've laid the groundwork by maintaining the proper distance. He thinks he has to follow you. He's not expecting you to move toward him and punch or to make him miss by a quick slip and countering. When you've finished punching, angle out, jab out or roll out and re-create your range.

Getting in and out without getting hit takes practice. It's best to develop more than one way to exit. Doing the same thing again and again will give your opponent a better chance of catching you (see the *Angles* chapter).

Two maneuvers not listed in *Angles* are the rollout and jab-out. After entering the boxing zone and punching, you can roll out by dropping straight down, simultaneously pushing your back foot out, sliding your front foot back and rising to an on guard stance. A jab-out entails throwing a jab as you pull your back foot out. The jab keeps your opponent from following you with a punch.

"Don't pull straight back" is a major truism in boxing. That's because your opponent can time you with a punch knowing where you're going to be — straight back from where you were. So it's important to change your head position, either left, right or down or by jabbing out.

Rollout — Simultaneously lowering and stepping back with the rear foot, then rising and stepping back with the front foot. By lowering, Alan is making himself a smaller, moving target more difficult to hit as he leaves the boxing zone.

3 4

In and out with a jab or jab-out — Throwing a jab on the way out prevents an opponent from punching you as you exit.

3  **4**

7

4

Fourth Commandment: Obey the laws of punching and punch power

There are two rules for every punch.

1. Finish the punch where it started — next to your chin on the same line at the same speed. I call it "retracing your punch." Full extension should be referred to as "impact position" not the "end" of your punch. Because, as stated, the end of your punch is where it began — at the chin.

2. The non-throwing hand should touch your chin. Defense is most important when you're punching for two simple reasons — you're in range to be hit and the punch itself creates an opening for your opponent to attack.

And there are two rules for power punching.

1. Pivot the foot of the hand you're throwing.

2. Transfer your weight through the punch.

That's it!

Let's examine each law a little closer. Say you and your opponent throw a jab at the same time. You "bow and arrow" yours by dropping your right hand. He, however, keeps his right hand to his chin. Everything else being equal, who do you think is going to score and who will get hit?

Anybody can protect himself while not being aggressive. It's not hard to protect yourself if that's all your
worried about. But that's not the name of the game.
The name of the game is "hit and not get hit." Or, to
take that a step further, "hit and make him pay for
trying to hit you." Now your boxing, baby!

Here's the trick to obeying the laws: Every time you
throw a punch, you must think your opponent is going
to try to hit you back. Through proper retracing
(finishing) of your punches, you won't be as timid to
let your hands go. This is because your expecting it, so
you're not surprised. If it doesn't come, then you're all
the more happy. This will give your punching laws
more meaning. Keep in mind that it's a "race back to
your face." Most knockouts occur when both boxers
are throwing a punch at the same time. It's the boxer
who doesn't obey the law who pays the price.

Punching power comes from the ground up. Every
coach in the world, no matter what sport, will tell you
that power comes from your hips. Your hips are the
"generator" that transfers the energy from the ground
through your body and out your punch. Your pivoting
foot acts as a plug in a socket. When your foot is
turned, the power comes on and the weight is trans-
ferred. Of course, there are people who have exceptional power that defies logic. I knew a boxer who
couldn't lift his body weight, but could bruise me even
when I wore a super body protector. Exceptional
punching power is God-given, but through proper technique, we can all maximize our potential.

Protecting the chin — Every punch should finish where it started — next to the chin.

The non-throwing hand stays glued to the chin.

Power punching — Alan pivots the foot of his throwing side and transfers the weight of his entire body through a straight right (above) and a left hook on the next page. Note the powerful thrust of shoulders and hips from start to finish in both sequences.

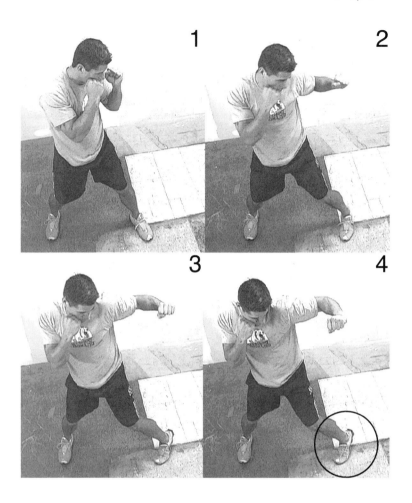

5

**Fifth Commandment:
Make the jab your best punch**

The jab is the number one punch in boxing!

Let's review some of the basic reasons why. The jab is the catalyst for every other punch. Your power punches wouldn't have nearly the same effect without the jab. The jab is the queen in a chess game. It can move you in any direction. It can create openings, frustrate oncoming attacks and win fights more easily.

If your opponent takes away your jab, chances of winning are greatly reduced. If thrown effectively, your jab will be about 70 percent of your offense. This is because it's the safest punch to throw — it doesn't compromise your on guard stance. It's also the shortest punch because it comes from your lead side in a straight line.

There are several types of jabs. Some are fast, some powerful, some are used to start combinations and others are used for defensive purposes. No matter how you use it — as a rhythm maker or a rhythm breaker; as a distracter or a range finder — you must commit to it. The jab is essential to your boxing success.

The basic jab is thrown, with no wasted motion, directly from your chin to your opponent with a slight rotation of the hand (impact position is palm down). This adds snap, "sears" your opponent's skin and causes abrasions. Remember to finish the punch by bringing it back to your chin.

Here's an overview of some jabs.

1. Pesky jab — The pesky jab is used to break your opponent's rhythm, to frustrate him into bad decisions and to occupy his mind on matters other than his own offense. This can be done by peppering your opponent with quick jabs, using jab feints and doubling and tripling them up. Throwing a jab while moving in all directions keeps you upright.

2. Stiff jab — The stiff jab is a more offensive weapon. It should stop an opponent in his tracks if not back him up. It should be thrown with the shoulder behind it. It should be extended a fraction longer than a normal jab to put more force through it. It helps to think "punching through your opponent."

3. Splitter — The splitter is thrown with the thumb up. This helps the punch slip through a well guarded opponent. It may also be used to "pot shot" your opponent since he won't be expecting it.

4. Upper jab — The upper is a sly, effective punch. It can snap your opponent's head up, which makes it easier to land the right hand. It's effective because it comes in on an upward line just below peripheral vision. It's a quick backward snap of the hand, and you'll be amazed how strong it can be. It's thrown like a seesaw — as your right shoulder lowers, your left shoulder rises and levers your left under the chin of an unsuspecting opponent. Be sure you know how to "pic" off the right hand with your left shoulder before trying it.

5. Blinder — The blinder jab is used to "blind" your opponent momentarily. The jab is held up and brought back without punching. It's a way to hide your intentions, like moving off to one side to get a better angle for your right hand.

There you have it. Make sure that with all of these techniques, your chin is tucked and your right hand is held next to your chin. Quickly returning to your on guard stance is critical.

1 **2**

1 **2**

Straight punches —The jab begins and ends next to the chin. Always on a straight line — like looking down the barrel of a rifle.

3   4

3   4

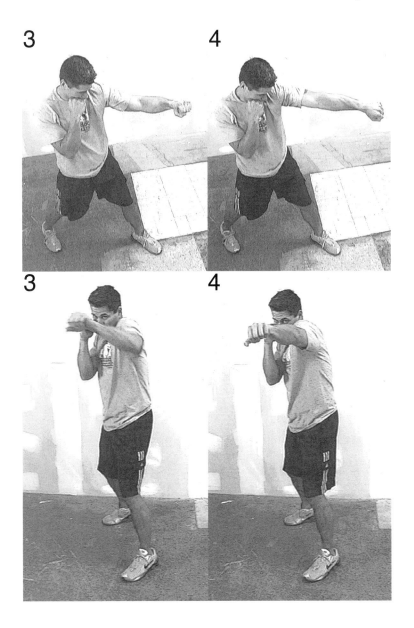

The jab

Punch path — Check out the sequence from 1 through 4 and then backward from 4 through 1. The punch is delivered and returned along the exact same path.

Telegraphing a jab — Raising the elbow is wasted motion and indicates or telegraphs your intention to throw a jab.

Jab body —The key to body punching is lowering yourself so that your shoulders line up with the target. Merely punching down from a regular stance has too little power over too great a distance.

Protected from counter — His chin is buried behind shoulder and arm.

The jab

3 **4**

Ideal form — The punch and its power shoot in a straight line when legs lower the upper body. Unlike the punch below.

Bad form — Punching down is not the way to effectively attack the body. And notice the exposed head!

6

Besides the jab and jab body, there are eight more punches you need to know!

The most important punch in boxing, the jab, was covered in Chapter 5. Remember, your lead hand is the closest and will make the quicker punch to your opponent. Throw it directly at your opponent with no wasted motion. It's also the hand you should feint with the most.

The granddaddy of all power punches is the straight right or right cross (orthodox for right rear power punchers). There are a few reasons boxers feel more comfortable throwing the right hand (power hand). First of all, it's your dominant hand. Most people do everything with their dominant hand — throw, eat, write and swing. So it's no surprise that it's the hand you're most comfortable punching with. Plus, it gives you the feeling of having your body behind it because everything is moving forward.

That's not the case with the left hook. The left hook is thrown with your body weight going from front to back, away from your opponent.

Let's look at power punching a little closer. First, always punch through your opponent. I always say, "aim one inch past your target." And, of course, the rules of power punching apply — pivot the foot of the hand you're throwing and transfer your weight.

Keep in mind that the greater the reward, the greater the risk! Now is the time your "laws of punching" come into play. If you miss a punch, you might become easy prey for a counterpunch.

Obey the laws! A properly thrown right hand starts from the ground up! As you begin to throw the right, your right foot starts to pivot, which brings the knee inward as the weight shift begins. As the energy travels up from a simultaneous rotation of your hips and shoulders (having a strong midsection also adds energy), it is delivered with as much force as possible. Your left side acts as a brace and should be strong. Staring down the barrel of your extended right arm is a good way to describe impact position. At impact, your palm rotates toward the ground while your chin remains tucked throughout. Finish by retracing your right arm back to its proper on guard position.

Punch mechanics

Following are sequences and captions describing the eight major punches other than the jab and jab body.

Straight right 2
Straight right body 2b
Left hook 3
Left hook body 3b
Right hook 4
Right hook body 4b
Left uppercut 5
Right uppercut 6

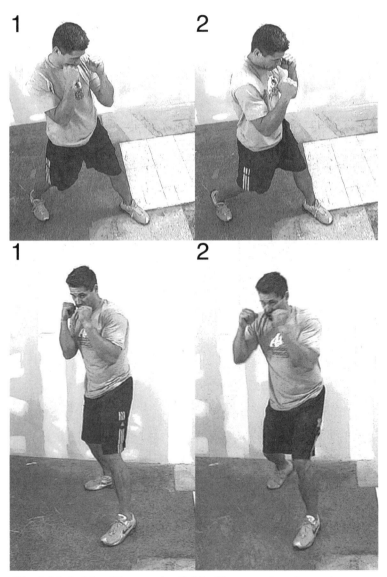

Straight right — Those who fight with a regular stance have the left foot forward. The rear hand is your right and it will deliver this power punch. Southpaws throw a straight left.

3 **4**
3 **4**

***The rear foot pivots and his entire body moves behind the
punch*** —Note the strong forward thrust of shoulders and hips.
This is a power punch!

Telegraphing a right —
Cocking the right before
delivery gives you away and
exposes your right side. This
punch launches from the chin!

Straight right punch profile — His elbow does not draw back! The punch travels from chin to target in a straight line.

Straight right body

3   4

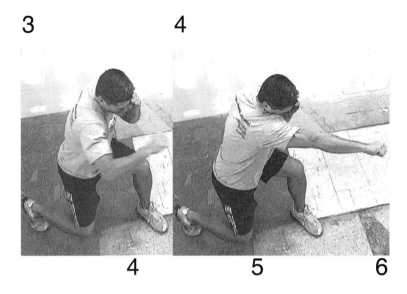

4   5   6

The way to get low —Say again: The key to body punching is lowering yourself so that your shoulders line up with the target. Merely punching down from a regular stance has too little power over too great a distance.

Punch mechanics

Straight right body in profile — Everything about this
sequence says, "Thrust forward!"

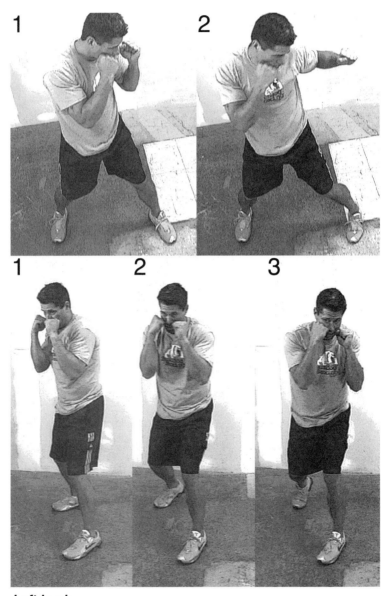

Left hook

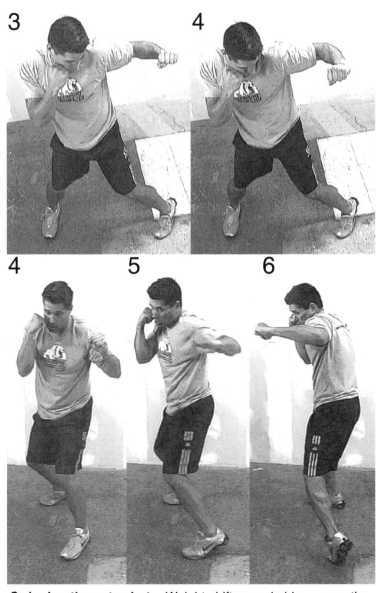

Swinging the gate shut —Weight shifts punchside — over the left foot. Everything — legs, hips, torso, shoulders, arm and fist — pivots in one piece. It's the complete body movement that makes this such a devastating power shot.

Palm positions — Palm should be in for a target outside the elbow and down for a target inside the elbow.

Telegraphing a left hook —
Keep your arm within your
frame. Dropping the arm
says, "Here comes my hook!"

Left hook body

3   4

4   5   6

Lowering to target —As he loads his left side, his legs bend to help bring arm and fist to body level. Shoulders and hips pivot over the left foot and bring the punch.

Left hook body profile

3   4

Right hook

3   4

4

Hooking the other way — The rear foot pivots because the rear hand delivers the blow. The last two images show palm down and palm in positions, respectively.

Right hook profile

Telegraphing a right hook — Like dropping your fist before a left hook, dropping your right arm before throwing the right hook is a clear signal to an opponent.

Right hook body

3   **4**

Hooking the other way — This time loading up the right side and pivoting body weight through the right foot and leg.

Right hook body profile

3   4

Punch mechanics

Left uppercut

Down and up — Alan brings his weight over to his left side, lowering himself by bending his knees. Throughout this shift, his left arm remains tight to his frame until he is ready to spring his uppercut by torquing his upper body and thrusting with his legs.

Left uppercut profile

3   **4**

Telegraphing an uppercut — Dropping the punching arm is a giveaway and diminishes the power of your punch. It's important to bring yourself into position by bending the legs and keeping your fist tight to your body. Fist, arm, shoulders, torso and legs move as one piece to launch an effective uppercut.

Right uppercut

4　　　　　5

4　　　　　5

No, this is not an arm punch!

Right uppercut profile

3   4

7

**Seventh Commandment:
Master the defenses against each punch
and know how to counter every attack**

*This book stresses the importance of countering
off your defense. "D" without "O" is a no-no!*

That being said, the first thing you have to learn is how
to make the incoming punch(es) miss. We've explored
the concept of range, but every now and then, you
must bring the fight in. Otherwise you'll always be out
of range yourself. Let's examine how to use blocks and
evasive moves inside the boxing zone. I prefer blocks
over slips because you're usually in position to hit
back! With slips you can very easily position yourself
out of a counterpunching position. Over-
slipping is quite common with new boxers. There are
several different maneuvers that fall under the category
of blocks.

Parries
A parry is an inside deflection of an incoming punch
with a short, quick tap using only your wrist and hand.
This may cause your opponent to become overex-
tended and vulnerable, thus giving you an opportunity.

Catching
Catching can be classified as a parry. When catching,
stay "chambered" — don't chase the punch away from
your face. As it comes toward you, apply just enough
pressure to redirect the punch away from its target.
Your hand should travel only 2 or 3 inches. If your chin
is properly tucked, and it's a stiff jab you're countering,

the backside of your glove will bounce off your fore-head. Your forearm should not pull away from the biceps. Think of "alligator arms" when parrying.

Body shot parries

Body shot parries are sometimes called pendulum blocks. A pendulum block is a sweeping motion down and away from your body.

Blocks

The goal is to put something in the way of the punch — like a glove, forearm or elbow in order to absorb the brunt of the blow.

Blocking head shots

Giving or rolling with head shots will make these kind of blocks more effective. When you place your glove against your head, you will feel the pressure of the blow but not the pain. I call it "answering the phone." Try to keep your elbow pointing down and your eyes on your opponent. Make sure there's no separation between your glove and face. Otherwise you'll end up hitting yourself. Adding a slight turn and weight shift with contact puts you in a position to throw a counter-punch of the same variety. If your opponent throws a right hand, you block and counter with your own right hand. When rolling with head shots, keep in mind not to shift more than a 60-40 weight transfer away from the punch.

Blocking body shots

There are two effective ways to block body shots. To block hooks to the body, "tip" the shoulder toward the incoming punch. This will keep you from pulling your

glove away from your face. To block straight shots, turn
your shoulders slightly so that your forearm and elbow
block the punch. Use the forearm closest to the punch,
which will probably be your lead (left) forearm.

Blocking uppercuts

Blocking the uppercut also is done two ways. One way
is to turn your forearm and glove into the punch. The
other is to cup the punch directly under your chin
with either glove hand. It's important to remember that
with all defensive maneuvers, your goal is to do as little
as possible to make the punch miss. Don't become fix-
ated on your defense. If you do, you will not be as
focused on your main goal — your offense!

Evasive moves

Evasive moves are just as important to learn. My
thinking is that against bigger guys, slips are more
effective than blocks because blocks still allow you to
feel the punches — absorbing lots of them from a big
man saps your energy. Evasive moves allow you to
really exploit aggressive boxers who overthrow their
punches. And it's frustrating to throw punches that
miss their mark. With all evasive moves, you must
match the intensity of the punch by "popping" your
defensive moves. That means the speed of head must
equal speed of hand.

Slips

Slips are initiated with a quick lateral or diagonal movement of the upper torso, mainly the head and neck.
Remember to make an opponent miss by the narrowest of margins. "Grazing the ear" is a popular way of
explaining it to boxers. A great slip grazes you in the

ear; a good slip flies over your shoulder, and a bad slip goes outside your shoulder. With the latter, you are in no position to throw a counter and are vulnerable because you're probably off balance as well. You should keep the shoulders level when slipping. Think of a clock with your opponent being 12 o'clock. You should bring your head to either 10 or 2 o'clock during a good slip. When you slip right, bring your left shoulder to the punch and your head to 2 o'clock. When you slip left, it's almost like you're throwing a right hand. Rotate your right shoulder at the punch and bring your head to 10 o'clock.

Ducks
Ducking is a broadly effective defensive tool because it works against hooks and straight punches to the head. The slip doesn't work against a hook because your head is on the same plane. A duck is performed by quickly bending the knees and leaning slightly forward. Do not look at the ground or you may get hit by the next punch you won't see coming.

Slides and rides
These are double moves to use against someone who throws a lot of combinations. A slide or bob is a half outside slip, half duck move. A ride or weave is half inside slip, half duck maneuver. Example: Your opponent throws a left hook, you first inside slip or ride the hook, then duck underneath it and return to your on guard stance.

Rock back
The rock back is a useful tool when combined with a slightly wider than shoulder-width stance. Don't rock

back with a narrower stance because your head will be over your back foot. You're basically stuck with no place to go. With a wider stance, the rock back will bring your head over your back knee. Because you are still in a balanced position, you have the ability to step with the back foot to avoid another punch or to reposition yourself.

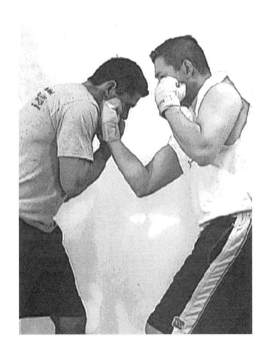

Universal punch key
Each punch has an assigned number that is recognized by boxers everywhere.

1	jab head
1b	jab body
2	right
2b	right body
3	left hook
3b	left hook body
4	right hook
4b	right hook body
5	left uppercut
6	right uppercut

Defender's Index
Defensive maneuvers for each major punch

1 Jab head
Catch
Parry
Opposite arm parry
Outside slip
Inside slip
Slide
Ride
Duck
Rock
Backstep

1b Jab body
Parry
Forearm block
Backstep

2 Straight right head
Glove block
Parry
Opposite arm parry
Shoulder block
Outside slip
Inside slip
Slide
Ride
Duck
Rock
Backstep

2b Straight right body
Forearm blocks right and left
Parry
Backstep

3 Left hook
Glove block
Duck
Ride
Rock
Backstep

3b Left hook body
Forearm block
Backstep

4 Right hook
Glove block
Ride
Duck
Rock
Backstep

4b Right hook body
Forearm block
Backstep

5 Left uppercut
Forearm blocks right and left
Glove blocks right and left
Outside slip
Inside slip
Rock
Backstep

6 Right uppercut
Same as left uppercut

> The following pages illustrate the defensive moves listed here.

Defending against jabs to the head

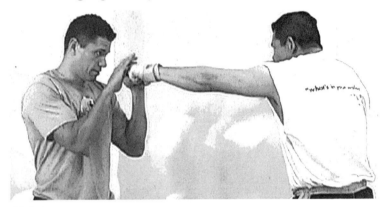

Catch

Parry   *Opposite arm parry*

Outside slip   *Inside slip*

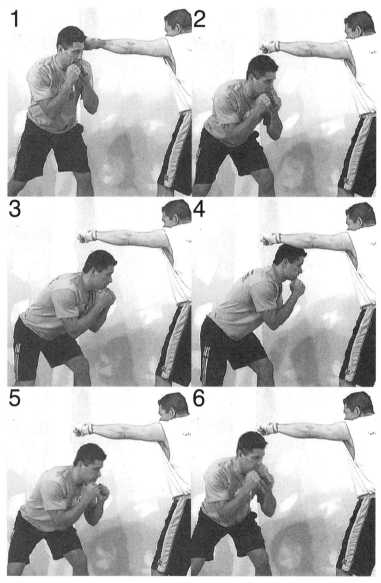

Slide

1

2

3

4

Ride

Duck

Rock

Backstep

Defending against jabs to the body

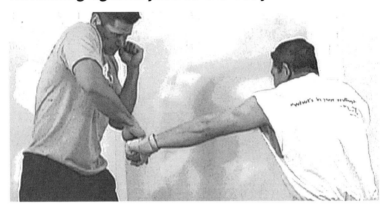

Parry

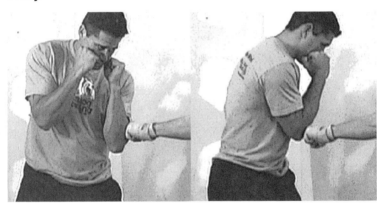

Forearm blocks

Backstep

Defending against straight rights to the head

Glove block

Parry   *Opposite arm parry*

Inside slip   *Outside slip*

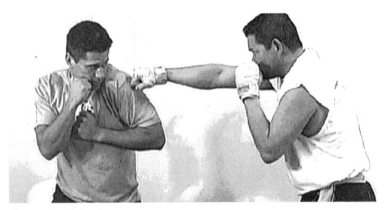

Shoulder block

Slide

Ride

Duck   **Rock**

Backstep

Defending against straight rights to the body

Forearm blocks

Parry   **Backstep**

Defending against left hooks to the head

Glove block   **Duck**

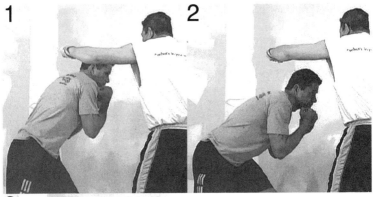

Ride

Rock   *Backstep*

Defending against left hooks to the body

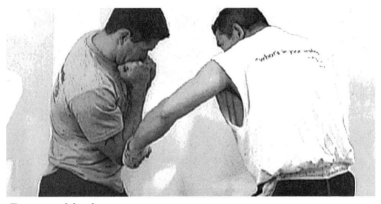

Forearm block

Backstep

Defending against right hooks to the head

Forearm block   **Duck**

Ride

Rock   **Backstep**

Defending against right hooks to the body

Forearm block

Backstep

Defending against left uppercuts*

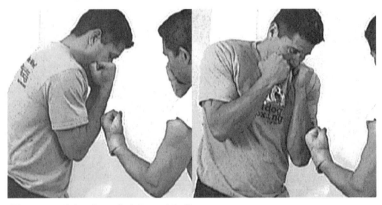

Forearm blocks, right and left

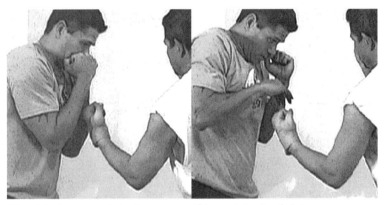

Double forearm block   *Glove block, right*

Glove block, left   *Rock back*

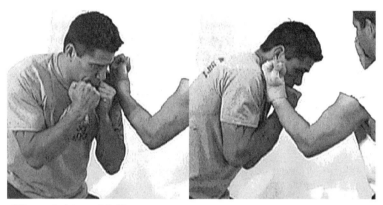

Slips, right and left

Backstep

*Defenses against right uppercuts are the same.

Counterpunching

Counterpunching
A counterpunch is the result of blending a defensive and offensive maneuver into one fluid act.

A counter takes your opponent's attack and uses it against him by exploiting the opening he created. Timing, speed and accuracy must all be in harmony.

Some general tips on counterpunching follow.

● Boxers are most vulnerable when punching because they are in range to be hit and are not in the on guard stance. The punch itself creates an opportunity. When your opponent throws a punch, he is not in an effective defensive position.

● Use a well-timed counter when you see or anticipate an opening or when you feel the pressure of your opponent's glove.

● Take advantage of the countering opportunities your opponent gives you to lower his punch output and to lessen their power.

● Boxers must be able to react in split seconds. To gain that reaction takes practice, practice and more practice! First, learn the proper punch to throw for each position you may be in with your opponent. And have a counter ready for every defensive move. Then have a counter with either hand in store for every offensive move.

● Rehearse these moves in front of a mirror as you shadowbox, in partner drills, in directed sparring, and of course, in open sparring. Make them a priority. Practice makes perfect and will result in good habits in the course of battle.

● The best way to minimize the openings you create when you counterpunch is to be active when you're in the boxing zone. Something should always be moving — your head, hands or feet — during and after you throw.

● Always be ready to counter a counter. To do so, you must be balanced and relaxed as you fight. This takes time and hard work to develop.

We've got combos!

On the next page is an index listing the proper defenses and counters for each of the ten major punches.

Universal punch key
Each punch has an assigned number that is recognized by boxers everywhere.

1	jab head
1b	jab body
2	right
2b	right body
3	left hook
3b	left hook body
4	right hook
4b	right hook body
5	left uppercut
6	right uppercut

The pages following the index illustrate each defensive maneuver and punch listed. The images read left to right, from top to bottom.

The first photo, usually framed, shows either Alan or Tony executing an appropriate defensive move. Next you'll see either Alan or Tony throwing the punch or punch combination (usually the latter) that make up the proper counter.

Counterpuncher's index

Proper defenses and counter combinations to the ten major punches

1 (Jab) vs.
Parry-1-2, 2-3
Opposite arm parry-1-2, 2-3
Outside slip-1-2, 2-3
Inside slip-1-2, 2b-3
Slide-1-2b, 2b-3b
Ride-1b-2, 2b-3b
Duck-1b-2, 2b-3
Rock-1-2, 2-3
Backstep-1-2, 2-3

1b (Jab Body) vs.
Parry-3-6, 4-5
Forearm block right-3-2, 6-3
Forearm block left-2-3, 5-4
Backstep-1-2, 2-3

2 (Straight Right) vs.
Parry-1-2, 2-3
Block-2-3, 3-6
Opposite arm parry-5-4, 2, 2-3
Outside slip-3b,4b, 2b-3b
Inside slip-1b-6, 6-3b
Slide-2b-3, 3b-2
Ride-1b-2, 2-b-3b
Duck-1-2, 2-3
Rock-1-2, 2-1
Backstep-1-2, 2-1

2b (Straight Right Body) vs.
Forearm block left-5-4, 2-3
Forearm block right-3-2, 2-3
Parry left-6-3, 3-2
Backstep-1-2, 2-1

3 (Left Hook) vs.
Glove block-3-2, 2-3
Duck-2b-3b, 1b-2b
Ride-1b-2, 2-3
Rock-2-3, 1-2
Backstep-1-2, 2-1

3b (Left Hook Body) vs.
Forearm block right-6-3, 3-6
Backstep-2-1, 1-2

4 (Right Hook) vs.
Glove block-6-3, 3-6
Ride-1b-2b, 2b-3
Duck-5-4, 6-3
Rock-6-3, 1-2
Backstep-1-2, 2-1

4b (Right Hook Body) vs.
Forearm block right-5-2, 2-3
Backstep-1-2, 6-3

5 (Left uppercut) vs.
Forearm block right-3-4, 6-3
Forearm block left-4-5, 3-2
Glove block right-3-2, 4-3
Glove block left-6-3, 3-2
Outside slip-4-5, 3-4
Inside slip-3-2, 2-3
Rock-2-3, 3-2
Backstep-1-2, 2-3

6 (Right uppercut) vs.
Forearm block right-3-6, 6-3
Forearm block left-5-4, 6-3
Glove block right-3-6, 2-3
Glove block left-6-3, 5-4
Outside slip-3b-2, 2-3b
Inside slip-6-3, 3-6
Rock-3-2, 2-3
Backstep-1-2, 2-1

Defenses and counters against the jab (1)

Parry, counter 1-2

Parry, counter 2-3

Opposite arm parry, counter 1-2

Opposite arm parry, counter 2-3

Outside slip, counter 1-2

Defense and counters

Outside slip, counter 2-3

Inside slip, counter 1-2

Inside slip, counter 2b-3

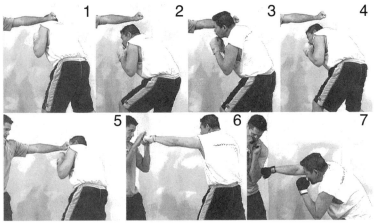

Slide, counter 1-2b

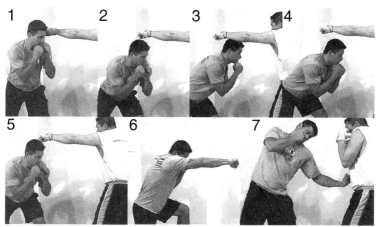

Slide, counter 2b-3b

Ride, counter 1b-2 or ...

... counter 2b-3b

Duck, counter 1b-2

Duck, counter 2b-3

Rock, counter 1-2

Rock, counter 2-3

Backstep, counter 1-2

Backstep, counter 2-3

Defenses and counters against the jab body (1b)

Parry, counter 3-6

Parry, counter 4-5

Forearm block right, counter 3-2

Forearm block right, counter 6-3

Forearm block left, counter 2-3

Forearm block left, counter 5-4

Backstep, counter 1-2

Backstep, counter 2-3

Defenses and counters against the straight right (2)

Parry, counter 1-2

Parry, counter 2-3

Block, counter 2-3

Block, counter 3-6

Opposite arm parry, counter 5-4

Opposite arm parry, counter 2

Opposite arm parry, counter 2-3

Outside slip, counter 3b

Outside slip, counter 4b

Outside slip, counter 2b-3b

Defense and counters

Inside slip, counter 1b-6

Inside slip, counter 6-3b

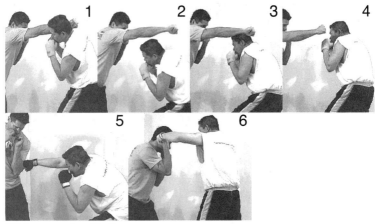

Slide, counter 2b-3 or ...

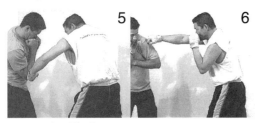

... counter 3b-2

130

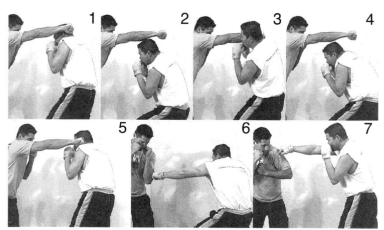

Ride, counter 1b-2 or ...

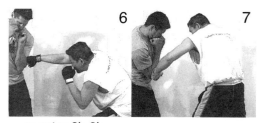

... counter 2b-3b

Duck, counter 1-2

Duck, counter 2-3

Rock, counter 1-2

Rock, counter 2-1

Backstep, counter 1-2

Backstep, counter 2-1

Defenses and counters against the right body (2b)

Forearm block left, counter 5-4

Forearm block left, counter 2-3

Forearm block right, counter 3-2

Forearm block right, counter 2-3

Parry left, counter 6-3

Parry left, counter 3-2

Backstep, counter 1-2

Backstep, counter 2-1

Defenses and counters against the left hook (3)

Glove block, counter 3-2

Glove block, counter 2-3

Duck, counter 2b-3b

Duck, counter 1b-2b

Rock, counter 2-3

Defense and counters

Rock, counter 1-2

Backstep, counter 1-2

Backstep, counter 2-1

Ride, counter 1b-2

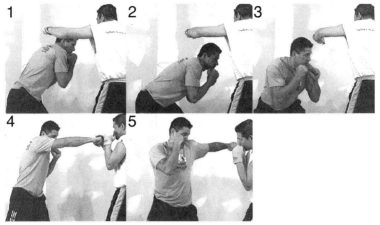

Ride, counter 2-3

Defenses and counters against left hook body (3b)

Forearm block right, counter 6-3

Forearm block right, counter 3-6

Backstep, counter 2-1

Backstep, counter 1-2

Defenses and counters against the right hook (4)

Glove block, counter 6-3

Glove block, counter 3-6

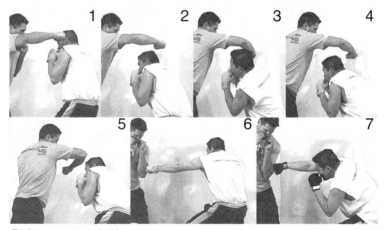

Ride, counter 1b-2b or ...

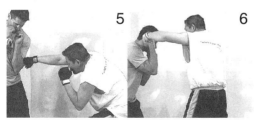

... counter 2b-3

Defense and counters

Duck, counter 5-4

Duck, counter 6-3

Rock, counter 6-3

Rock, counter 1-2

Backstep, counter 1-2

Backstep, counter 2-1

Defenses and counters against right hook body (4b)

Forearm block right, counter 5-2

Forearm block right, counter 2-3

Backstep, counter 1-2

Backstep, counter 6-3

Defenses and counters against the left uppercut (5)

Forearm block right, counter 3-4

Forearm block right, counter 6-3

Forearm block left, counter 4-5

Forearm block left, counter 3-2

Glove block right, counter 3-2

Glove block right, counter 4-3

Glove block left, counter 6-3

Glove block left, counter 3-2

Outside slip, counter 4-5

Outside slip, counter 3-4

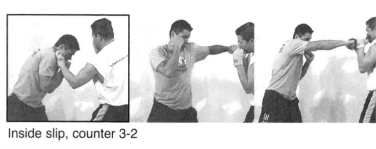

Inside slip, counter 3-2

Inside slip, counter 2-3

Rock, counter 2-3

Rock, counter 3-2

Backstep, counter 1-2

Defense and counters

Backstep, counter 2-3

Defenses and counters against the right uppercut (6)

Forearm block right, counter 3-6

Forearm block right, counter 6-3

Forearm block left, counter 5-4

Forearm block left, counter 6-3

Glove block right, counter 3-6

Glove block right, counter 2-3

Glove block left, counter 6-3

Glove block left, counter 5-4

Outside slip, counter 3b-2

Outside slip, counter 2-3b

Inside slip, counter 6-3

Inside slip, counter 3-6

Rock, counter 2-3

Rock, counter 3-2

Backstep, counter 1-2

Defense and counters

Backstep, counter 2-1

8 Angles

Eighth Commandment:
Angle in and out on different lines

Learning how to angle in and out will keep you from getting hit with more than one punch at a time.

Most great fighters in their prime never got hit with even two punches consecutively. That's because they knew the angles! Giving your opponent angles keeps him on the defensive. He has to keep lining you up to hit a target.

Most novice boxers move only in and out on a straight line. They are easy to hit because their opponents don't have to "find" them. They know where they're going to be. An angle is any deviation from this course. Going straight in then quickly stepping to either side is an angle. Angels are both offensive and defensive. An offensive angle is used when entering the boxing zone or when engaged. A defensive angle is an evasive tactic, used to move out or off center and to create openings.

V-step
Examples of offensive angles are the V-step and the cutoff step. The V-step resembles the letter "V" if you look at it from above. It's an in-and-out style where you attack your opponent at an angle, not head on. Before your opponent can adjust, you exit on a different line thus forming the letter V.

Cutoff step

The cutoff step can be used to "cut the ring off" by quickly stepping in the direction your opponent is moving. If you beat him to that spot, you momentarily stop his movement. An infighter usually uses this technique to hunt his opponent down. However, it can be used to attack and spin off or with a side step to create more openings without getting hit.

45 degree step

Defensive angles include the 45 degree step, 90 degree or triangle step, slide step and ride step. Forty-five degree steps are when you enter the boxing zone at an angle (taking away one of your opponent's hands) to avoid getting hit by a certain punch and to create more offensive opportunities. A 45 degree step is a good way to close the distance while slipping a punch. With the slip, you would step in 45 degrees with your lead foot.

90 degree step

The 90 degree step is executed by stepping in, then getting your next step almost even with the front foot of your opponent. This forms a 90 degree angle.

Slide step

The slide step is done in combo with an outside slip. Here, you step around your opponent while outside slipping his jab or straight right. This usually works best against his right because you're stepping with your lead foot first.

Ride step
The ride is done with an inside slip. After you inside slip either a jab, cross or hook, you duck and step to the outside of the punch and look for openings.

Inside angles
Angles are categorized as inside angles and outside angles. Inside angles are used as your initial move to the inside. From there you move to either side of your opponent, depending on the hand thrown, using ride steps or backing out using a 45 degree step. Examples of inside angles are ride steps (in to out) and 45 degree steps.

Outside angles
An outside angle is the opposite. Your first move brings you outside. From there you may want to work back inside using slide steps or stay off of center using a side step. Outside angles include slide steps (out to in), side steps, 90 degree steps and cutoff steps.

Remember, giving your opponent something different to look at always keeps them THINKING about hitting you, NOT ACTUALLY hitting you.

V-stepping to his right

3   4

V-stepping to his left. Stepping in at an angle then stepping out at an angle so his path forms a "V."

Cutting off to his left and delivering a left hook body.

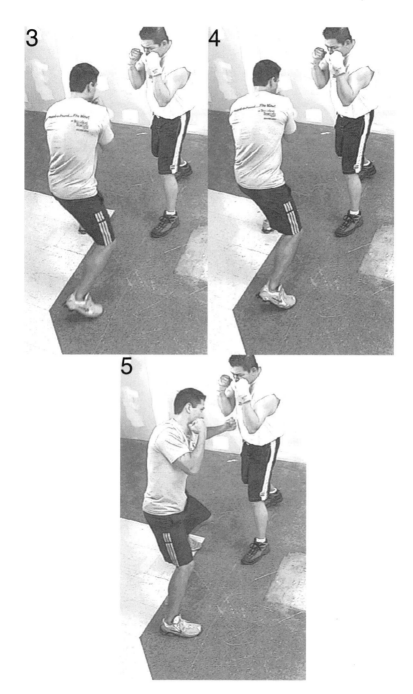

Cutting off to his right and finishing with a right hook body.

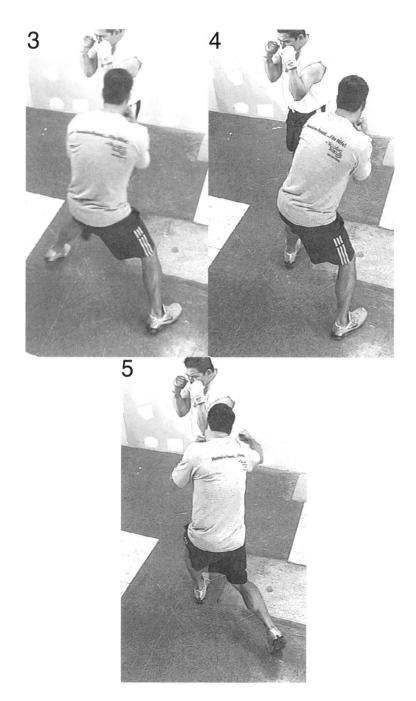

5

45 degree step — Angling left. Stepping in on a straight line and then stepping out and "off" at a 45 degree angle.

3   4

1　**2**

5

45 degree step opposite direction — Angling to his right. Stepping in straight and "off" at a 45 degree angle the other way.

3 **4**

90 degree or triangle step with lead jab — Stepping in with a jab and angling to his right. Punch options after creating the angle include right head, left hook body and left hook head, shown in that order.

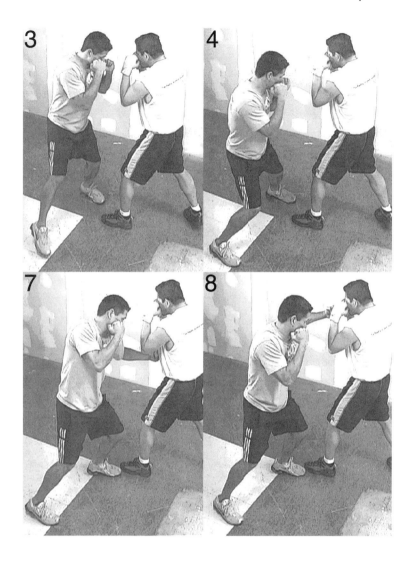

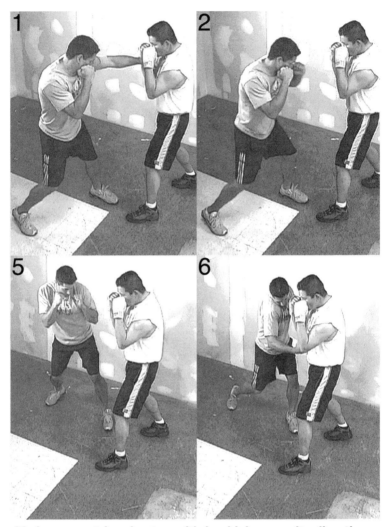

90 degree or triangle step with lead jab opposite direction
— Stepping in with a jab and stepping off to his left. Alan finishes with a right hook body, right hook head and left hook head.

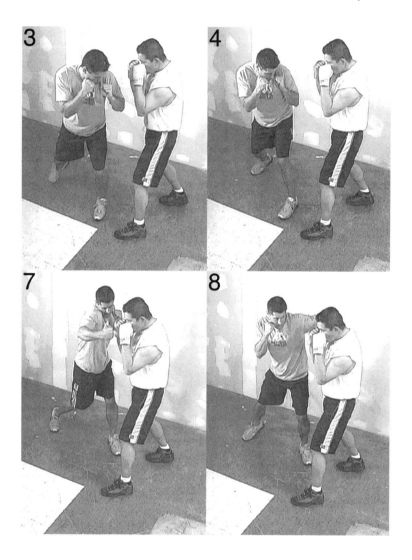

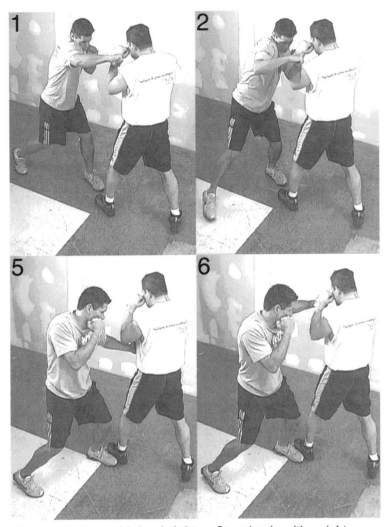

90 degree step with lead right — Stepping in with a right, stepping off to his right, finishing with a left hook body, left hook head and right head.

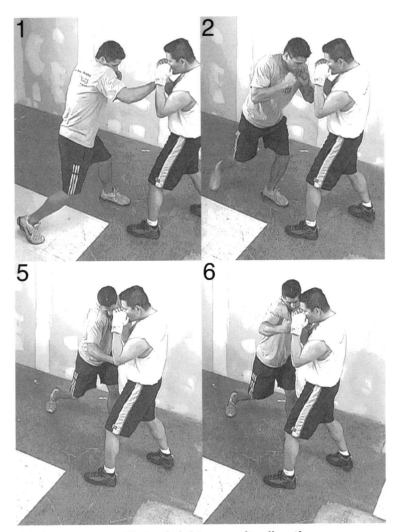

90 degree step with lead right opposite direction —
Stepping in with a right, stepping off to his left, finishing with a
right hook body, right hook head and left hook head.

Side step left with punches — Slipping a jab, stepping left and delivering a right body and a left hook body.

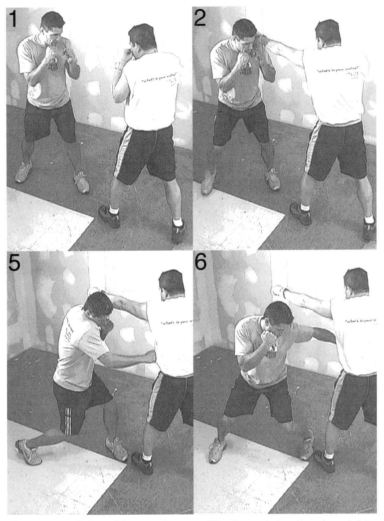

Side step right with punches — Slipping a jab, stepping right and delivering a right hook body and a left hook body.

Side step with pivot —
Sidestepping right and
pivoting with his left foot.

***Side step with pivot
opposite direction*** —
Sidestepping left and pivoting
with his left foot.

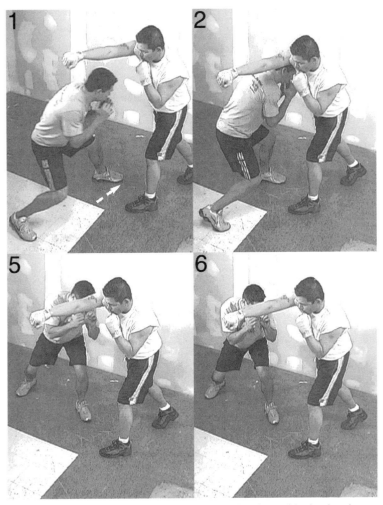

Ride spin — Riding under a right and pivoting with the lead stepping foot.

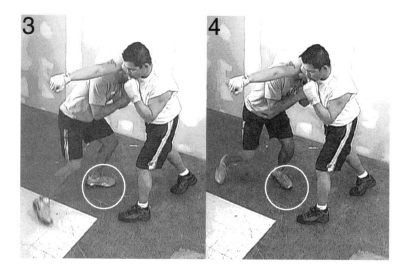

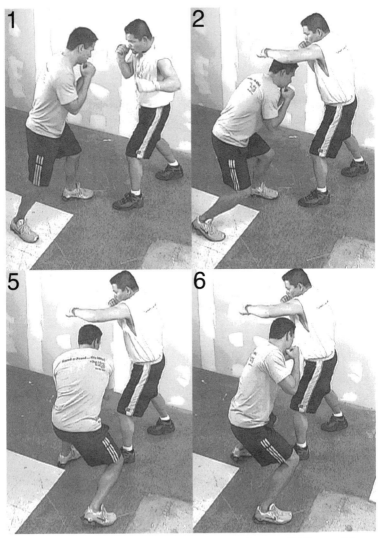

Ride spin opposite direction with punches — Riding to his right under a left hook by ducking and pivoting around his left foot. This angle gives him the opportunity to throw a left hook body, right head and left hook head shots, shown in that order.

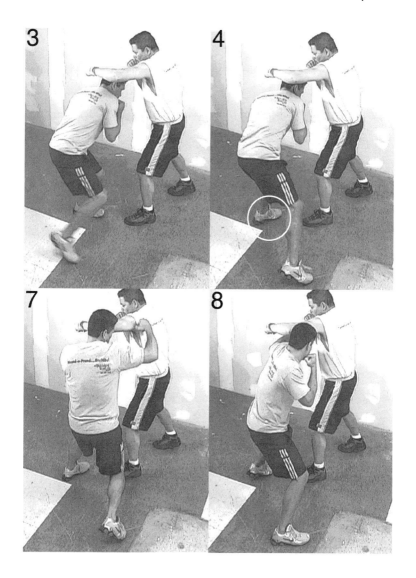

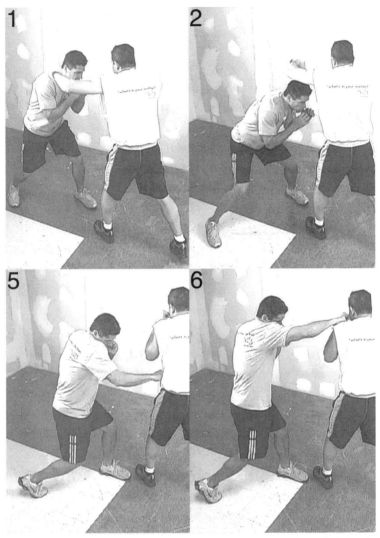

Ride step with punches — Riding to his right under a left hook by ducking and stepping. From this angle, he throws a right body, right head, left hook body and left hook head.

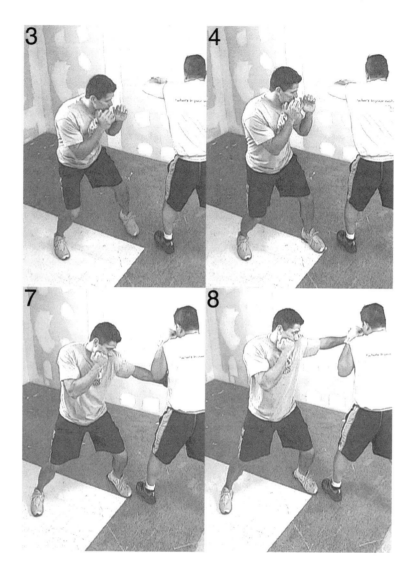

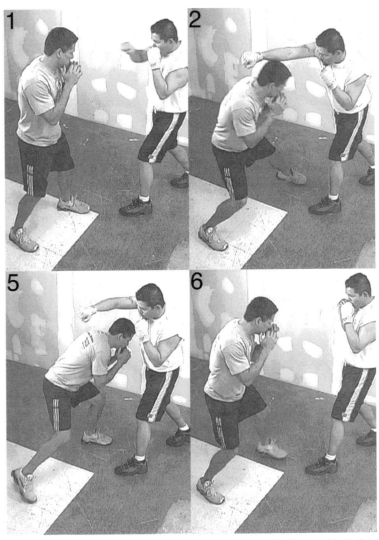

Ride step opposite direction, in and out — Riding to his left under a left hook by ducking and stepping and then stepping back out.

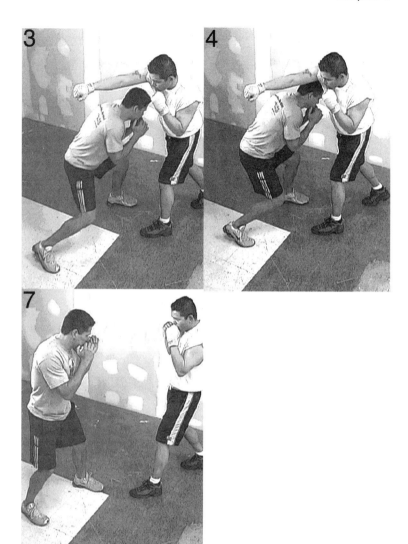

9

**Ninth Commandment:
Blend and master offensive and defensive
skills through focused sparring drills**

The best way to test yourself is to spar.

Sparring successfully entails correct application of fundamentals under pressure. Many armchair quarterbacks
criticize from outside the
ring, but they have no
idea of the difficulties
boxers face inside the
square circle. You will discover the truth of this
during your first sparring
session.

Let me start by saying
that sparring or any contact drill should be performed under
supervision. And you
shouldn't consider sparring until you have
gained proper punching mechanics and sound defense.
Good fundamentals cannot be rushed! Sparring should
always be taken seriously and should be about skill
building. It should rarely be a free for all. In order to
benefit from sparring, you must practice specific skills
so you can master the skills of punching, protecting
yourself, counterpunching and staying relaxed. This will
allow you to move into open sparring and competition.

Preparing to spar: Two-step sparring
Two-step sparring is when you and your partner each perform two offensive moves and two defensive moves. The most basic example is when you start by throwing a jab, your partner parries and throws a jab, you parry and throw another jab, your partner parries, throws a jab and you parry.

Level one is blocks only, level two is evasive moves, level three is a combination of both. I like to start with blocks because they keep you in a better position to hit back. That is, you remain in an on guard stance at the proper position, distance and balance to counterpunch. Evasive moves may disrupt your guard, move you out of a good countering position and even upset your balance.

The sky is the limit when it comes to two-step drills. Use a variety of punches, defensive moves and angles in your training. Practice simple moves and gradually build to more complex ones. Start with single-punch closed-chain drills (knowing what punch is coming). Next try combination closed-chain drills (knowing what punch combinations are coming). Then move to single open-chain drills (not knowing what punch is coming), and finally combination open-chain drills (not knowing what combinations are coming).

Two-step training drills
Closed chain
Level 1
Blocks

1. Jab (parry) — Jab (parry) x 2

2. Right cross (block) — Right cross (block) x 2

3. Left hook (block) — Left hook (block) x 2

4. Jab (parry), cross (block) — Jab (parry), cross (block) x 2

5. Jab (parry), hook (block) — Jab (parry), hook (block) x 2

Start with two-punch combinations. After you master these, add more punches to your combinations.

Level 2
Evasive moves

1. Jab (outside slip) — Jab (outside slip) x 2

2. Right cross (outside slip) — Right cross (outside slip) x 2

3. Left hook (duck) — Left hook (duck) x 2

4. Double jab (inside, outside slips) — Double jab (inside, outside slips) x 2

5. Jab (outside slip), cross (inside slip) — Jab (outside slip), cross (inside slip) x 2

Level 3
Blocks and
evasive moves

1. Jab (parry) — Jab (duck) x 2

2. Right cross (inside slip) — Right cross (shoulder block) x 2

3. Left hook (ride) — Left hook (block) x 2

4. Double jab (outside slip, inside slip) x 2

— Double jab (parry, slide) x 2

5. Jab (parry), left hook (ride) — Jab (duck), left hook (block) x 2

Two-step training drills / open chain

Now try open-chain drilling (not knowing what punches are coming). Break it down as before, start with one punch versus blocks, evasive moves, combo "D" moves and finally combo punching.

Level 1 — Blocks

Jab (parry), right cross (block), right uppercut (block), left hook (block)

Level 2 — Evasive moves

Right cross (outside slip), left hook (ride) ...

... right hook body (1/2 step), jab (duck)

Level 3 — Blocks and evasive moves

Jab (rock), left hook (1/2 step), jab body (block), left hook body (block)

Once again, the sky is the limit. The five most commonly used punches are the jab, right cross, left hook head, left hook body and right uppercut. Use these punches the most in your training, but don't neglect any one punch.

The right hook body and head are used least. The right hook is a wide punch thrown from your back side and must travel a great distance to reach your target. Uppercuts can be problematic since they are usually telegraphed by dropping your hand away from your face — something an observant opponent will see and easily counter.

Directed sparring

This is the last step before advancing to open sparring. Each boxer is given a set of directions and focuses on a specific skill. Both boxers may move at top speed, but they must work as a team. Examples of directed sparring include offense versus defense, jab versus jab, lead hand only, power hand only, body punching only, angle in/out and punch, boxer versus puncher... the list is as long as your imagination.

Combinations in open chain

Jab (outside slip), right cross (ride) ...

... ride continued   Left hook (block), right uppercut (block)

Left hook (block), left hook (duck), left hook body (block), right hook (ride) ...

... ride continued

Right cross (block), left hook body (block), right hook body (block)

Open sparring

This is the final frontier before competition. In sparring, quality is much more important than quantity. Open sparring involves everything — throwing combinations, defense, counterpunching and studying your opponent. Both boxers should stay controlled.

It's not often that you and your sparring partner will be at the same skill level. If you are much better than your opponent, work on your weaknesses. If you are not as good as your sparring partner, ask him to take it easy. The last you thing need is to develop bad habits because you fear getting hurt. Here are some basic rules for sparring with different skill levels.

Sparring with a novice

Make sure he's relaxed and he feels he can ask you questions before, during and after the session. Work on your defense. Work on your weaknesses. Don't embarrass or intimidate your partner. Don't get too flashy or overconfident. Stay within the boxing zone so that he can throw punches. Capitalize on his mistakes, but don't make him pay too high a price. Instead, teach him the consequences of bad technique. Stay focused and relaxed. Remember the feeling of confidence and the power of a positive attitude.

Sparring with someone better

Sparring with someone better than you can teach you more than sparring with someone of lesser skill. It can elevate your intensity, focus and skill level. When sparring stronger boxers, talk to them about your experience and what you want to get out of the sparring session. Try to maintain your composure in the ring.

You will get hit! When you do, don't retaliate with anger. The session will escalate into a fight, and your opponent might punish you more. Remember to show respect. Work tough for your sparring partner —that is how you will gain respect.

Getting in "boxing shape"

Work until you or your partner cannot spar with good form. Round robin sparring is a good way to build your boxing fitness. This way you can go hard and get rounds off. It's important that you train like you compete. Going easy all the time will make you go easy when it counts. You're only as good as your training.

How many rounds? If you box four two-minute rounds in amateurs, you should train four or five three-minute rounds in the gym. Sparring rounds that last longer than your performance time will make the performance rounds easier. Also, cutting down on the rest interval will build endurance.

Always challenge your boxing fitness. Don't coast during rounds. Good sparring sessions should remain active, explosive and intense throughout the entire session. Practice like you intend to perform and get in "boxing shape." There's a big difference between being in shape and boxing shape. Boxing shape requires both aerobic and anaerobic fitness. You can't successfully train by running marathons or sprints only. It must be a combination of the two while under duress. That's why it's imperative that you spar to get into boxing shape. It's called the S.A.I.D. principle — Specific Adaptation for Imposed Demands.

Last words

● Spar because you want to improve skills, have fun, and of course, be successful. Your intent should never be to hurt someone. It's hard enough as it is.

● Realistic expectations of your performance are important. Mistakes (many of them) will happen. Reward your effort and correct technique.

● Get comfortable with the idea of getting hit and hitting someone early on. It's easier said than done!

● Get familiar with your opponent. Talk to him.

● Know the style you want to start with. It may change according to your opponent, but try to stick with it for a while.

● Make sure your partner knows the plan and pace of your sparring workout. We recommend that beginners spar half speed.

● Establish a pace that benefits you. Don't throw punches carelessly — you'll only punch yourself out.

● We recommend you jab and keep a good distance from your opponent so that you can study him. Notice his tendencies when you jab and feint (hand, head and shoulder movements as if to punch). If your opponent reacts with the same move two or three times in a row, it's probably a habit — then you can capitalize on it.

● Stay under control and relaxed. Remember, there's no shame in stopping the action if you feel yourself getting overwhelmed.

10 Having a plan

Tenth Commandment:
Follow a plan every round — be it workout, sparring or competition

This final chapter deals with workout plans, reading styles and winning strategies.

Failing to plan is planning to fail. Most fights are won and lost before boxers step into the ring. To use a football analogy, look at Bill Bellichick, head coach of the world champion New England Patriots. Most observers will tell you that he never really had the fastest, strongest, toughest team that won all those Super Bowls. What he did have was a better game plan. In studying his opponents strengths and weaknesses (as well as his own), he was able to create mismatches and put his team in a position to win. All (and granted it's a big all) the players had to do was execute.

Having a plan means more than planning for a single fight. It means having a plan each and every time you set foot in a gym. Your daily workouts should be challenging and fresh so that you're not going through the motions. You need to learn how to be a good observer when you're in and outside the ring. Watching different styles from outside the ropes can be as valuable as experiencing them inside. Improving your observation skills will improve your boxing skills! Remember, we're talking about the Sweet Science. Boxing isn't fighting. Boxing is boxing! You must have a plan!

In the first part of this chapter I'll show you winning workouts that have withstood the test of time. There is a method to the madness.

Following are three workouts that will maximize your time spent at the gym. It's important to use these workouts in this specific order. I've also included a generic workout so that you may plug in your own drills and ideas.

Try to use each workout plan for at least 6-8 weeks. Visualize being successful and stay focused throughout the entire workout.

Coaching points for all workouts
1. Always warm up. Stretch and jump rope first.
2. Use rhythmic movement in every round.
3. Make sure something is always moving — hands, head and feet.
4. Have a goal in mind for every round.
5. Visualize your opponent trying to hit you in every move you make.

Training equipment

You will need wraps and bag gloves. Also the maize or slip ball for head movement, the double-end bag for evasive moves and punching accuracy, a jump rope, and of course, a heavy bag. A ring is great for shadow-boxing because it makes your workouts realistic. But a large open space will do. Find a full length mirror in order to review your technique. Finally, make sure you wear properly fitting headgear, mouthpiece, sparring gloves and groin protection for sparring.

Slipping the maize.

Practice punching accuracy and evasive moves with the double-end bag.

See pages 213-216 for ten variations of jumping rope.

Work combinations and most everything else on the trusty heavy bag.

Workout #1 — 20 rounds

Shadowboxing and mirror training — 5 rounds
1 — In front of a mirror, practice stance, guard, rhythm and footwork including advance, retreat, lateral, in-out and in-off. Everything starts with stance and footwork. Move forward, back, left and right. In-out means straight in and out. In-off means in and 45 degree step out going left and right. You do it in front of a mirror so you can evaluate your form.

2 — In front of the mirror, practice punching mechanics including the jab 1, straight right or cross 2, left hook 3, left hook body 3b and right uppercut 6. Emphasize technique. These punches are the most used and most effective punches in boxing. Emphasizing technique means you should slow down a little and over-exaggerate your pivots.

3 — In front of the mirror, practice defensive moves including blocks and evasive moves. Before anything else, learn how to block and slip the jab 1, straight right 2, left hook 3, left hook body 3b and right uppercut 6.

4 — In front of the mirror, practice counterpunching with a single punch off a defensive move. Work these counters off each defensive move: 1, 2, 3, 3b and 6.

5 — This round is for open shadowboxing in the ring and style development. Practice what you've been working on in the first four rounds. Let it flow. Doing it in the ring makes it more real.

Heavy bag work — 8 rounds
6 and 7 — Practice punching mechanics. Combine the work you did in the first two rounds of mirror training (but not in front of a mirror — focus on the bag). Emphasize technique. Work out as if you were giving a seminar to 100 people on how to properly hit the bag with good technique.

8 and 9 — Work defense and counterpunching. Combine the work you did in rounds three and four. Usually 80-85 percent of heavy bag work is offensive minded. Make it 50 percent here. Visualize the bag hitting you. Defend and counter!

10 and 11 — Practice style role-playing: Boxer and infighter. Mimic the boxer and infighter styles. The bag is the boxer and you are the infighter and vice versa.

12 and 13 — These are open rounds for style development. Everything goes here. Just work!

Double-end bag — 2 rounds
14 — Work basic punches with footwork. If you're new to the double-end bag, try hitting it with just your open hand until you become proficient. Don't try to do too much, keep it simple.

15 — Practice defensive moves. Hit the bag enough to get it going, then work primarily on your defense.

Maize bag — 2 rounds
16 — Practice slips. You want the swinging bag to miss by the narrowest of margins. Remember this rule of thumb: If the bag flies over your shoulder — good, outside your shoulder — bad.

17 — Counterpunching. Make him miss, make him pay!

Partnership drills — 3 rounds
18 — Single punch shut-out drills. The goal is to make your opponent miss with every punch he throws by using a defensive move.

19 — Footwork drills. This is like dancing with your partner. Here you are learning range and rhythm. Take turns trying to find each other's rhythm.

20 — Counterpunching. D without O is a no-no. Counterpunch your partner.

Workout #2 — 23 rounds

Shadowboxing and mirror training — 5 rounds
1 — In front of the mirror, practice stance, guard, rhythm, footwork, directional steps and angles. Start with the basics, then work on angles and pivots. Work on angles and pivots without throwing punches first. Use the mirror to correct yourself. Remember, what you see is what your opponent sees.

2 — In front of the mirror, practice the mechanics of all 10 punches. Emphasize speed. In other words, pretend you're a lightweight — someone with exceptional technique and speed.

3 — In front of the mirror, work lead drills, counterpunching in combinations. Throw a punch and imagine your opponent countering it, then you counter his counter. Also do this without the mirror.

4 and 5 — Work on style development in the ring with an emphasis on fluidity. Try to look natural. Let everything flow nice and easy.

Heavy bag work — 8 rounds
6 and 7 — Practice punching mechanics. Combine the first two rounds of mirror training. Emphasize speed technique.

8 and 9 — Lead drills. Counterpunch off defensive moves and make angles. Initiate the action by throwing a punch, making a defensive move, then immediately countering and clearing (angling out).

10 and 11 — Style role-play: Boxer and infighter. Emphasize speed. You and the bag have different styles. Work outside your comfort zone.

12 and 13 — Open, style development. Let it go! See what style you naturally assume and improve on it.

Double-end bag — 2 rounds
14 — Throw punches off angles. Use lots of angles including the 45 and 90 degree steps and cutoffs.

15 — Work with a defensive emphasis. Get a little closer. This will force you to defend against the bag.

Maize bag — 2 rounds
16 — Slips with footwork. Slip and step at the same time. This closes the distance to your opponent.

17 — Counterpunching with angles. Make the bag miss by using your feet and countering.

Partner and pad drills. Closed chain — 3 rounds
18 — Shut out drills and combinations. Shut him out by not allowing him to score. Throw combinations.

19 — Footwork drills in the ring. Get comfortable with the ring surface. Practice pivots, angles and getting off the ropes.

20 — Two-step drills. Take turns leading, countering and countering the counter. Work on only a couple each workout.

Directed sparring and sparring — 3 rounds
21 through 23 — Offense versus defense. During each round start at 25 percent speed, increasing to 50, 75 and finally 100 percent or full speed. The fighter working on his defense should try to capture the same feeling of being relaxed and successful at 100 percent as he did at 25 percent.

Workout #3 — 26 rounds

Shadowboxing and mirror training — 5 rounds
1 — In front of the mirror, work stance, guard, rhythm, footwork, directional steps and angles. Try different styles. Use the mirror to evaluate yourself.

2 — In front of the mirror, practice punching mechanics. Emphasize attacks on scoring areas. Scoring areas are legal places to hit an opponent where a boxer gets credit. High = head, low = body, inside = front of face or body, outside = side of face or body. Think about all the possible scoring areas — High and low, inside and outside. Attack them all. Most combos should attack at least two different scoring areas.

3 — Defense and movement in the ring. Focus on fluidity and smoothness. Mix in a variety of moves using your head, hands and feet. Use the ring — work on and off the ropes, in and out of corners and in the middle.

4 and 5 — Open, style development in the ring. Move like you're actually in a bout — focused and intense. Throw lots of punches. Use the ring to simulate a fight or use any large area where you can move around.

Heavy bag work — 8 rounds
6 and 7 — Punching mechanics. Perfect technique on all punches.

8 and 9 — Counterpunching. Emphasize angles. Use angles to set up scoring opportunities. Throw in combinations.

10 and 11 — Style role-play. Boxer and infighter. Emphasize power. Work on different styles. Picture yourself as Joe Frazier, Muhammad Ali and Mike Tyson.

12 and 13 — Open, develop personal style. Work your style while staying under control and relaxed.

Double-end bag — 2 rounds
14 — Punching in combinations and movement. With gloves on, mix in an array of speed and power.
15 — Defensive emphasis. Get into the rhythm of the bag. Be fast!

Maize bag — 2 rounds
16 — Slips with footwork. Slip and step simultaneously, work to both sides.
17 — Punching while moving. Slip to one side and throw either hand as lead. Repeat on the other side. Build to combos.

Partner / pad drills / closed chain — 3 rounds
18 — Shut-out drills and counterpunching. Keep your partner from hitting you while he throws combinations.
19 — Angles on attack, engaged. Stay inside the boxing zone and use angles to avoid getting hit and to set up shots.
20 — Two-step drills. Work two or three sets on combos, both giving and receiving, then angle out and circle to reset drill.

Directed sparring and sparring — 6 rounds
21 through 26 — Sparring. Emphasis on strategy and timing. Boxing is a thinking man's game. Have a plan and stick to it!

General workout

As you can see, boxing should never be boring or mindless. Here is a list to help you create your own winning workout. Put in the drills you like and learned.

Jump rope	Warm up	2-4 rounds
Shadowboxing/ mirror	Footwork Punches Defense Counterpunching Open, style	3-5 rounds
Heavy bag	Combinations Speed Power Non-stop punching	6-8 rounds
Double-end bag	Combinations Movement: Moving head or upper body	2 rounds
Maize bag	Evasive moves Counterpunching	2 rounds
Partner drills	Shut out drills Combinations Counterpunching Movement / footwork: Angles, rhythm and range	4 rounds
Directed sparring/ Sparring	Style Combinations Speed Power Fluidity	4 rounds

Staying within this guideline will enable you to develop all the skills needed to be successful in the ring. The variety will keep it interesting. Always focus on the skills you want to develop and keep your intensity at a high level. Remember, each round should have a goal or emphasis.

Jumping rope

Ten variations.

Feet together, forward and backward

One foot at a time

Knees up high

Double skipping (two turns of rope per jump)

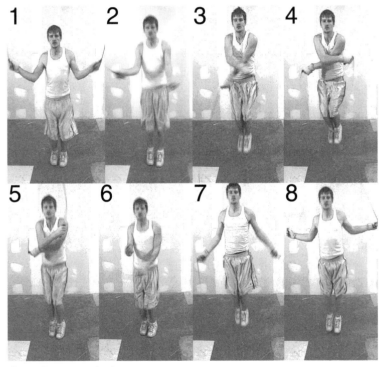

Crossing arms in front

Side to side

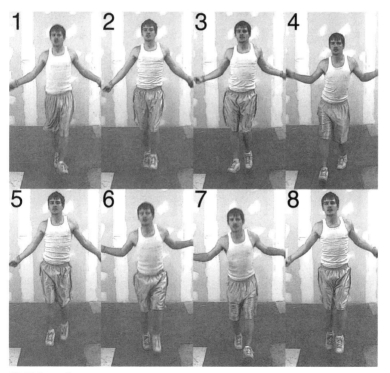

Split jumping

Having a plan

Shifting rope side to side

Boxer's shuffle

Resources

EQUIPMENT
Everlast
718-993-0100

Ringside
1-877-4-BOXING
www.ringside.com

Title
1-800-999-1213
www.titleboxing.com

MAGAZINES
The Boxing Record Book
Fight Fax, Inc.
PO Box 896
Sicklerville, NJ 08081-0896
609-782-8868

Boxing USA
United States Amateur Boxing,
Inc. (USA Boxing)
One Olympic Plaza
Colorado Springs, CO 80909
719-578-4506

Boxing (year)
KO Magazine
Ring
Ring Boxing Almanac
  and Book of Facts
Ring Extra
Ring Presents
World Boxing
All are published by
London Publishing Company
7002 West Butler Pike
Ambler, PA 19002-5147
215-643-6385

Hispanics in Boxing
R. Paniagua, Incorporated
155 East 42nd Street
Suite 206
New York, NY 10017-5618
212-983-4444

International Boxing Digest
(Boxing Illustrated)
International Sports Ltd.
530 Fifth Avenue
Suite 430
New York, NY 10036
212-730-1374

Ring Rhetoric
American Association for the
Improvement of Boxing
86 Fletcher Avenue
Mount Vernon, NY 10552-3319
914-664-4571

MUSEUMS
International Boxing
Hall of Fame
Hall of Fame Drive
PO Box 425
Canastota, NY 13032
315-697-7095
Fax 315-697-5356

ORGANIZATIONS
Amateur
Golden Gloves
Association
of America
1503 Linda Lane
Hutchinson, KS 67502
615-522-5885

Fax 615-544-3829

International Amateur
Boxing Association
135 Westervelt Place
Creskill, NJ 07626
201-567-3117

Knights Boxing
Team International
2350 Ventura Road
Smyrna, GA 30080-1327
770-432-3632
Fax 770-528-2132

United States Amateur
Boxing, Inc. (USA Boxing)
One Olympic Plaza
Colorado Springs, CO 80909
719-578-4506
Fax: 719-632-3426
usaboxing@aol.com

Professional
International Boxing
Federation (IBF)
134 Evergreen Place, 9th Floor
East Orange, NJ 07018
201-414-0300

North American
Boxing Federation
14340 Sundance Drive
Reno, NV 89511
702-853-1236
Fax 702-853-1724

World Boxing
Association (WBA)

www.wbaonline.com

World Boxing Council (WBC)
Genova 33, Oficina 503
Colonia Juarez
Cuauhtemoc
06600 Mexico City, DF, Mexico

World Boxing
Organization (WBO)
412 Colorado Avenue
Aurora, IL 60506
630-897-4765
Fax 630-897-1134

Other boxing organizations
American Association
for the Improvement of Boxing
36 Fletcher Avenue
Mount Vernon, NY 10552
914-664-4571

International Boxing
Writers Association
50 Mary Street
Tappan, NY 10983
914-359-6334

International Veteran
Boxers Association
35 Brady Avenue
New Rochelle, NY 10805
914-235-6820

Fax 914-654-9785

VIDEOS
Ringside
They carry all the boxing videos known to man. Check out their catalog: 913-888-1719.

WEB SITES
Amateur boxing news
http://www.usaboxing.org
USA Boxing is the national governing body for amateur boxing in the United States.

International Boxing Hall of Fame
http://www.ibhof.com/

News, articles, schedules and more.
http://www.boxinginsider.com

http://www.boxingline.com

http://espn.go.com/boxing

http://www.fightnews.com

http://www.hbo.com/boxing

http://www.houseofboxing.com

http://www.showtimeonline.com/scboxing/

http://www.toprank.com/

Women's boxing
http://www.femboxer.com/

Index

More great boxing books from Tracks

Our boxing books are among the best-selling boxing instructional guides on earth because they are affordable and loaded with information you should know. Books are available through all major bookstores and booksellers on the Internet.

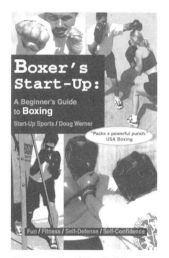

Boxer's Start-Up
The essential guide for beginner's. $11.95
Werner / Lachica

Fighting Fit
Advanced workouts.
$11.95
Werner / Lachica

Boxing Mastery
Technique and Tactics.
$11.95
Hatmaker / Werner

Author / Coach

Alan Lachica is a certified USA Amateur Boxing coach and owner of Bulldog Boxing Gyms. This is the third boxing guide he has authored or co-authored. Lachica's first two books, *Boxer's Start-Up* and *Fighting Fit,* have been among the top selling boxing guides since 2000. He also co-authored  *Fitness Training for Girls* in 2001. As an amateur boxer, he won over 90 percent of his bouts. His boxing exhibitions have been featured on local and national television including *Eye on America* (CBS News). He is a graduate of Cal State Long Beach and Ashworth College where he earned a degree in criminal justice. He currently lives in South Carolina with wife Lynne and daughter Camryn and serves as a Spartanburg County Sheriff's Deputy.